Dot TO Dot
IN THE Sky

Dot to Dot in the Sky

STORIES IN THE STARS

Joan Hinz

whitecap
Vancouver / Toronto

Edited by Elizabeth McLean
Cover design by Roberta Batchelor
Illustrations by Chao Yu and Jue Wang
Interior design by Warren Clark

Printed and bound in Hong Kong

National Library of Canada Cataloguing in Publication Data
Hinz, Joan, 1963–
    Dot to dot in the sky

    Includes index
    ISBN 1-55285-182-6

    1. Constellations—Juvenile literature. I. Yu, Chao, 1963–
II. Wang, Jue, 1958–
III. Title.
QB801.7.H56 2001   j523.8'022'3   C2001-910975-X

The publisher acknowledges the support of the Canada Council for the Arts and the Cultural Services Branch of the Government of British Columbia for our publishing program. We acknowledge the financial support of the Government of Canada through the Book Publishing Industry Development Program for our publishing activities.

For Les, Matthew, Gina, and Amy,
my partners in stargazing

Acknowledgments

I would like to recognize the assistance
given by Frank Florian, community astronomer at the
Odyssium (Edmonton Space & Science Centre), and
Douglas Hube, professor emeritus at the University of
Alberta and former national president (1994–96)
of the Royal Astronomical Society of Canada.

Contents

Look Way Up!

The vast sky around us sparkles from the distant light of hundreds of billions of stars. Each one is a burning ball of gas, like our sun. The stars look like twinkling spots of light in the black sky because they are so far away.

About 5000 stars can be seen without the aid of a telescope. On a clear, moonless night, away from city lights, you might see up to 2500 stars from one spot. A telescope will reveal even more.

People have always been fascinated by the night sky. Long ago, they imagined they could see pictures shaped out of stars. They called these pictures constellations, with the Sumerians naming the first ones around 4000 B.C.

In about 150 A.D., the astronomer Ptolemy published a list of 48 constellations. All but one of them still carries the same name today.

Space Notes

☆ People started observing stars in the Middle East at least 5000 years ago.

☆ Early astronomers saw the same star patterns we see today.

☆ We see the universe as it was in the past. If a star is 50 light years away, we see it as it looked 50 years ago, because that's how long it has taken the light to reach us.

Now there are 88 official constellations. They have not changed since the International Astronomical Union formally defined them in 1930.

Many of the constellations represent the mythical figures created by ancient cultures. Early Greeks and Romans believed in many different gods. They made up stories about gods, heroes, and animals to explain things they did not understand, such as disease, storms, and the changing seasons. Some of their tales also describe how these mythical characters came to be placed in the sky as stars. After conquering the Greeks, the Romans accepted the Greek myths as their own, but changed the gods' names.

Some of the mythical characters are easy to see in the star patterns, while other constellations require you to use a great deal of imagination to see their namesakes.

To begin your search, you only need to find a single constellation. Then just follow the arrows and connect the dots to spot many more.

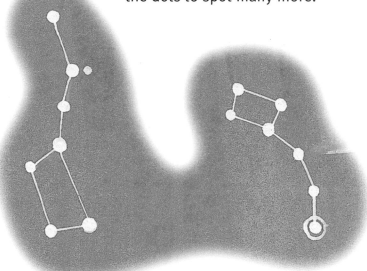

Connecting the Dots

Use the dot-to-dot patterns on the following pages to spot your first constellations. These star groups were selected as some of the easier ones to discover. Several contain luminous (bright) stars, while others appear closer together, and others are located near a more distinct constellation. The constellations are presented in an order that will make it easy to jump from one star group to another.

When you look at the Constellation Chart, you will notice that some stars are drawn larger than others, to represent the brighter stars. It will be easier to find the entire constellation if you look for the brightest stars first.

You do not have to count or see every star in the picture to have found a constellation. Some stars are fainter than others because they are less luminous or they are farther away. Even a crescent moon can cast enough light to make some stars invisible.

Circumpolar constellations are groups of stars that can be seen year round. As you travel farther north, more stars become circumpolar. Other stars can best be seen at different times of the year. Look for the season listed after the name of each constellation—this will tell you the best season for early evening viewing. The constellation may also be spotted in other seasons, but at a different time of night.

A constellation may appear at a different angle than shown, because of your location and the rotation of the Earth. Each season can change its orientation. You may have to try tilting your head to make it easier to spot the shape of a constellation, if it's not at the same angle as the picture.

Space Notes

☆ Astronomy is the science of studying the universe.

☆ Astronomers learn about the color, brightness, temperature, and composition of stars by studying light from space.

☆ Air is always moving. When light shines through the moving air currents of the Earth's atmosphere, the light bends, and the stars look as if they are twinkling. Observatories are often built on mountaintops because it is easier to see distant objects through the thinner air.

Equipment List:
Eyes and Flashlight!

The great thing about searching for constellations is that you do not need any special equipment. A telescope or binoculars are handy when looking at single stars, but are not much use when looking at a group. It is best to locate the stars of a constellation with the naked eye.

To begin, all you need are:
- a cloudless, dark night
- the constellation charts in this book
- comfortable clothes for your season and climate
- a flashlight
- red cellophane or a piece of red plastic from a shopping bag
- an elastic band

Cover the bulb end of your flashlight with the red cellophane or plastic, then use the elastic band to secure the plastic around the light. Now when you look from the chart to the sky, your eyes will focus more easily.

The light-sensitive part of your eye—the retina—contains rod and cone cells, named for their shape. Cone cells are mainly in the center of the retina and help you to see things in color and in fine detail. Rod cells are chiefly on the outer edge of your retina, and are more sensitive to faint light, as well as to movement.

If you are looking for a faint star, turn your head a bit and look out of the corner of your eye. The star that you could not see when you looked straight ahead may be easier to see now!

Space Notes

☆ When your pupils enlarge at night, more light enters your eyes, allowing you to see fainter stars.

☆ Stars near the horizon are harder to see because of atmospheric extinction. The denser air near the horizon absorbs some of the starlight.

☆ Light pollution results when outdoor lights shine in all directions, instead of on one specific area. This can create enough glare to reduce the number of stars you see.

Ursa Major
(ER-suh MAY-jer)

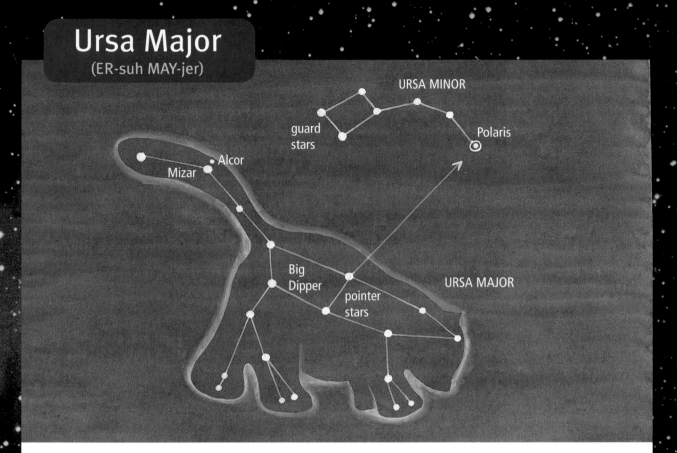

URSA MINOR

guard stars

Polaris

Mizar

Alcor

Big Dipper

pointer stars

URSA MAJOR

The Great Bear
(circumpolar)

Why is there a bear in the sky? According to Greek legend, it started with Zeus, the king of the gods. Zeus loved a nymph named Callisto, who lived in the mountains and liked to hunt.

Zeus's wife, Hera, was jealous of Callisto and turned her into a bear. Even though Callisto looked like a bear, she thought like a person. When she walked through the forest, Callisto was afraid of the other wild animals, but she was also afraid of hunters.

One day when her son Arcas was out hunting, he saw a bear and did not know it was his mother. As Arcas lifted his spear to kill the bear, Zeus looked down from Mount Olympus. He saved Callisto by turning Arcas into a bear also, then reached down and grabbed the tails of the two bears. He had to pull hard to lift them into the heavens and, as he pulled, their tails stretched. That is why the bears in the sky have longer tails than the bears we see on Earth. The tail of Arcas (Ursa Minor) is longer than that of Callisto (Ursa Major) because it stretches as he swings around Polaris, the North Star.

Hera was very angry when she saw the two bears in the sky. She complained to her friends who ruled the ocean and asked them to put the bears in a pen, so they couldn't move around much. Oceanus, one of the ocean gods, and his wife, Tethys, felt sorry for Hera and agreed to stop the bears from traveling. In the northern latitudes, the bears never set below the horizon and never go into the sea.

In North America, Micmac lore tells a different legend about a bear. It is represented by the four stars that make up the bowl of the Big Dipper, which is part of Ursa Major. The bear is not alone—the three stars in the handle of the Dipper are hunters. The second hunter from the end is looking forward to cooking the bear meat. He carries a pot, which you can see as the small star next to him. Another four hunters may be represented in the nearby constellation of Boötes.

After a winter of sleep, the bear wakes up and crawls out of his den in Corona Borealis, the Northern Crown. The seven warriors hunt the bear all spring and throughout the summer.

The hunters follow the bear across the northern horizon until autumn, when they finally catch up and kill the bear. The bear's skeleton stays in the sky until spring, but its spirit returns to the den. Every spring, a new bear emerges to be pursued by the hunters. You can tell the bear has been killed because every fall blood spills down and turns the leaves red.

☆ The Earth spins from west to east, which makes the stars look as if they're traveling east to west. However, it's the Earth, not the stars, that rotate. Stars do move, but if you watched the same one for a hundred years, you wouldn't be able to tell.

☆ At the equator, sky watchers can see all the constellations. The stars in the east rise straight up and sink directly down in the western sky.

Where Is It?

The Big Dipper is the starting point for finding several constellations because it is one of the easiest star patterns to spot. Face north, look up, and search the northern sky for the seven distinct stars that form the Big Dipper. The two stars on the opposite side from the handle are called the pointer stars.

Once you've found the Big Dipper, connect the dots to see the rest of Ursa Major.

If you can't see the Big Dipper this way, follow the instructions under Ursa Minor (the Little Bear) to find the Little Dipper. One dipper can always help you locate the other.

Star groups like the Big Dipper are only part of a constellation. They are called asterisms.

A CLOSER LOOK

The entire constellation of Ursa Major can be seen year round from Canada and the northern United States. At least some of Ursa Major is visible all year from any location in the U.S. It can also be seen from the equator.

The Big Dipper has also been seen as a plow, a bushel measure, and a long-tailed skunk. In Germany, people saw the Big Dipper as a wagon and three horses, while in Britain it was King Arthur's chariot. The Romans saw seven oxen driven by Arcturus, the brightest star in the constellation Boötes.

Before the American Civil War, slaves sang a song that explained how to follow the Drinking Gourd to freedom in the north. By calling the Big Dipper the Drinking Gourd, they could share directions without slave owners understanding the song's real meaning.

The second star from the end of the handle is really two stars, known as Mizar—the horse, and Alcor—the rider. Some people can see the pair without binoculars. Ancient Arabs tested their eyesight by trying to see two stars.

Of the seven stars that make up the Big Dipper, five are part of a star cluster—a group of stars close to each other in space and born at the same time, out of the same material.

Polaris

URSA MINOR

Little
Dipper

guard
stars

Ursa Minor
(ER-suh MY-ner)

The Little Bear
(circumpolar)

Ursa Minor is an important constellation because it is home to Polaris, the North Star, and to the Little Dipper. The two stars on the end of the Dipper are called the guard stars and Ursa Minor needs them! When the bears got old, Ursa Major became jealous of Ursa Minor's pole star. She wanted Polaris for herself because it was as bright as her other stars.

Fortunately, the bigger bear was never able to steal the pole star because the "guard stars" are between Polaris and Ursa Major.

Where Is It?

If you were at the north pole and looked straight up, Polaris would be the star almost directly overhead. You can pinpoint the North Star by following the arrow from the Big Dipper (see Ursa Major), or try to locate it by first finding your location on a world map. The parallel lines running east and west show your latitude—the distance in degrees above or below the equator. Find the latitude line closest to where you live, and note the number of degrees.

Now face north and hold your fist straight out in front of you, palm sideways. The distance from your index knuckle to the knuckle of your little finger equals about 10 degrees. Now go up, hand over hand with your fists, counting by tens to the same number of degrees as your latitude. You will be pointing to the North Star, at the end of the Little Dipper's handle.

Polaris and the guard stars are brighter than the rest of the Dipper. Once you see them, connect the dots to find the rest of the stars in Ursa Minor.

A CLOSER LOOK

Polaris is about 50 times larger than our sun, but at 600 light years away, it is much farther from the Earth.

At 150 million kilometres (93 million miles) away, the Sun is the closest star to the Earth. Light from the Sun takes just eight minutes to reach our planet.

When you face Polaris, you are looking due north. In the past, sailors relied on the positions of the stars as a guide when they could no longer see land. Star, or celestial, navigation is still an important skill for sailors.

The constellations close to Polaris are circumpolar stars from viewpoints in northern latitudes, including most of North America. These constellations never set.

Draco
(DRAY-koe)

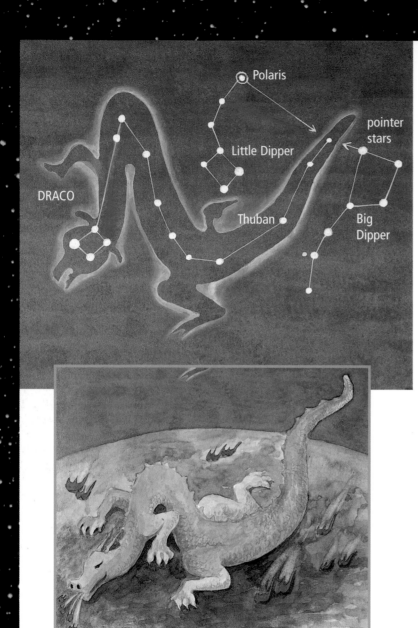

Polaris

pointer stars

Little Dipper

DRACO

Thuban

Big Dipper

The Dragon
(circumpolar)

In one Greek myth, Hera, the queen of the gods, had a special garden containing a grove of trees, where golden apples grew. Beautiful maidens called nymphs lived in the garden.

Their job was to guard the apples—but the nymphs loved the golden apples too much. Instead of protecting the beautiful fruit, they began to steal it for themselves! When Hera found out, she sent a dragon with a hundred heads to guard the apples.

One day the monstrous dragon was approached by Hercules, a hero who was half-god and half-mortal. As part of his quest to become immortal, Hercules needed to steal a golden apple, but the only way to get an apple was to defeat the dragon. He slew the beast and Draco was set in the sky.

In another Greek myth, a 10-year war had been raging between the giant Titans and the gods of Mount Olympus. Horrible monsters rose out of a fiery volcano to fight against the gods.

One of the monsters picked up a dragon and threw it at Athena, the goddess of arts, crafts, and war. Instead of feeling terror, Athena reached out, caught the dragon, and tossed him into the sky.

As the dragon flew up, his body twisted and turned until it became tied up in knots. Now the dragon sleeps in the northern sky with his head hanging down.

Where Is It?

Draco is a long, winding constellation. Many of its stars are faint, but it is not hard to find Draco because he lives near the bears. The end of Draco's tail begins between Polaris and the pointer stars in the Big Dipper (the two stars on the side of the bowl away from the handle). He winds his way right around the other side of the Little Dipper.

Space Notes

☆ People first started studying the stars to learn how to forecast the weather and changing seasons.

☆ Around 400 B.C., an early Greek astronomer named Eudoxus suggested that the Earth was motionless and surrounded by clear spheres. He thought the stars were attached to the largest sphere, and the Sun and planets were each attached to different inner spheres.

A Closer Look

The third star from the end of Draco's tail is called Thuban. It was the pole star to the ancient Egyptians in 3000 B.C.

Hindu myths describe this constellation as an alligator.

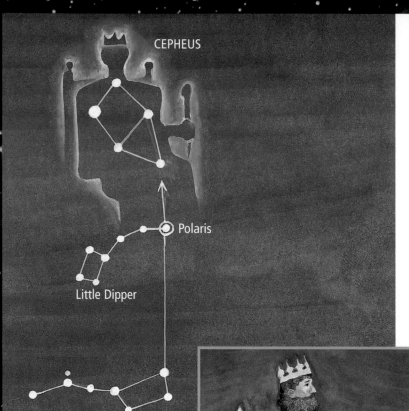

CEPHEUS

Polaris

Little Dipper

Big Dipper

Cepheus
(SEE-fee-us)

The King
(circumpolar)

The story of Cepheus is told in a Greek myth about the king of Ethiopia. He was married to Cassiopeia and they had a daughter named Andromeda. Both the queen and her daughter were truly beautiful, which made Cassiopeia proud.

One day, Cassiopeia made a big mistake. She bragged that they were even more beautiful than the nymphs living in the sea. The nymphs heard her bragging and wanted the queen to be punished. They went to Poseidon, god of the sea, and told him about Cassiopeia's insulting words. Poseidon agreed to revenge them and sent Cetus, the whale, to Ethiopia. The ferocious whale began attacking and killing people and animals, destroying the land near the ocean.

The people begged Cepheus to stop the beast, but the king did not know what to do. He asked for help from an oracle—a person with magical powers who could interpret the gods' wishes. The oracle told Cepheus the only way to stop the whale would be to chain Andromeda to a rock on the shore, as a sacrifice to Cetus.

Feeling helpless, Cepheus left his daughter by the water. He did not want to give her up, but knew it was the only way to save the people in his kingdom.

When Cetus saw the beautiful princess, he began swimming towards the rock. The whale was nearing shore when Perseus, a son of Zeus, flew over on winged sandals. Perseus was so impressed by Andromeda's beauty, he told the king he would kill the sea monster if he could have two things—

a kingdom, and Andromeda for his wife. Cepheus agreed and Perseus attacked the whale with his sword. Twisting in the water, the whale died and sank to the bottom of the ocean.

Cepheus and Cassiopeia were so relieved that the whale was dead and Andromeda was safe, they immediately made plans to celebrate with a feast.

Where Is It?

The constellation Cepheus is not very bright, but it is easy to find because of its shape. It looks like a square attached to a triangle, or like the outline of a house. Follow a line from the pointer stars in the Big Dipper (the two stars on the side of the bowl away from the handle), through Polaris to the tip of the house's roof.

Space Notes

☆ There are four basic types of galaxies: spiral, barred spiral, elliptical, and irregular.

☆ All the stars visible to the unaided eye are in the Milky Way galaxy, usually considered a spiral galaxy—a disk shape surrounded by spiraling arms. The Milky Way may actually be a barred spiral, meaning that it may have a more elongated center, with spiraling arms. Elliptical galaxies have a smooth, oval center with no spiral structure, and irregular galaxies have no obvious structure.

A CLOSER LOOK

In 1951, an American astronomer named William Morgan observed the brightness of the stars in Cepheus, Cassiopeia, and Perseus. He realized they must all be about the same distance away, which led to his discovery of the outer-most main spiral arm of the Milky Way galaxy—the Perseus Arm.

Now you see me, now you don't! Mira is a variable star in the constellation of Cetus. Its brightness changes, so you can only see it with the naked eye during part of the year.

Cassiopeia
(Cass-ee-uh-PEE-uh)

CASSIOPEIA

Gamma

CEPHEUS

The Queen
(circumpolar)

When Cassiopeia died, she was placed among the stars, next to her husband, King Cepheus. The sea nymphs did not think it was fair that the queen was honored with a place in the sky, for they had never forgiven her for bragging that she was more beautiful than them.

Once again, the nymphs went to Poseidon to complain. To make them happy, the sea god tilted the throne where Cassiopeia sat.

For half the night the queen is sitting up straight and proper, but for the rest of the night she does not look very majestic as she almost falls off her throne.

Where Is It?

Cassiopeia may be a queen, but she looks more like the letter W. She can be spotted by imagining a line starting at the bottom of the triangle in Cepheus. Continue the line farther into the Milky Way (see the Constellation Chart) to connect with the W.

Imagine that the lowest three stars in the illustration of Cassiopeia are an arrowhead.

They point to the Andromeda galaxy, shown as M31 in the Constellation Chart. The Andromeda galaxy is the only other galaxy besides the Milky Way that can be seen without a lens.

A CLOSER LOOK

- The Arab people thought Cassiopeia looked like a kneeling camel.

- The middle star, Gamma, is an irregular variable star. Observing stars that change in brightness is a great way to train your eyes to recognize faint sky objects. To observe a variable star, compare its brightness to nearby stars over a few weeks.

Space Notes

☆ The Earth is located in the Milky Way galaxy, which contains some 200 billion stars that look close together, but are actually far apart. The stars form a band of light stretching across the sky. Try looking for the Milky Way along Cassiopeia and Cygnus, the Swan.

☆ The Milky Way is about 100,000 light years across. It looks like a sparkly white cloud because our eyes cannot make out all the individual stars.

☆ The stars in the Milky Way travel around its center. The whole galaxy is also spinning.

☆ When you look into the black part of the night sky, you are looking away from the disk and spiral arms of the galaxy.

☆ If you look at the Andromeda galaxy, you are looking at the farthest object the naked eye can see. Its light takes more than 2 million years to reach the Earth.

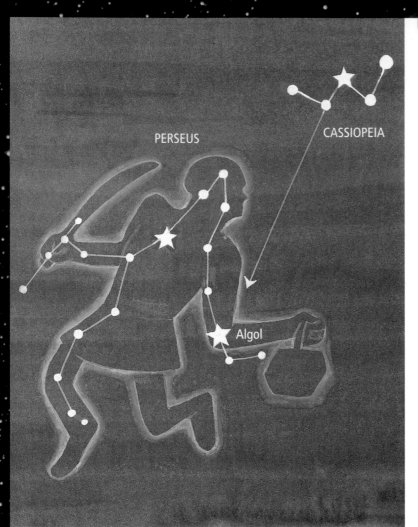

PERSEUS

CASSIOPEIA

Algol

Perseus
(PUR-see-us)

The Hero
(circumpolar)

When Perseus flew over the maiden Andromeda, he was on his way back from Medusa's home. Although she had once been a beautiful woman, Medusa had been turned into a hideous monster. Snakes grew out of her head instead of hair, making her so frightening to meet that anyone who even glanced at her was immediately turned to stone.

Perseus's mother, Danaë, wanted him to kill the unsightly creature. Taking a bright shield and winged shoes, Perseus flew to the place where Medusa lived and found her asleep. He used the bright shield like a mirror, watching the reflection of the monster but never looking right at her. Carefully sneaking up, Perseus cut off Medusa's head, then dropped it in a sack.

Perseus still had the sack with him when he saved Andromeda from Cetus the whale. After the rescue, there was a great party—and one problem. Cepheus had promised Perseus that he could marry his daughter, but he had also once promised his brother, Phineus, that he could marry Andromeda.

During the celebration Phineus tried to take an unwilling Andromeda away. Cepheus did not know what to do, so he hid, while Perseus challenged Phineus to fight. Phineus had an army on his side, and Perseus was losing the battle. To end the fighting, Perseus shouted to his friends to cover their eyes. When he pulled Medusa's head out of the sack, all his enemies were turned to stone.

Perseus and Andromeda were married, and spent many blissful years together. When they died, Athena placed them among the stars, where Perseus still protects Andromeda from Cetus, the whale who chases her across the sky.

Where Is It?

Follow the Milky Way (see the Constellation Chart) like a road. Start at Cassiopeia and the next constellation will be Perseus. If your area is not dark enough for you to see the Milky Way, just connect the dots from Cassiopeia to Perseus.

A CLOSER LOOK

The star Algol is sometimes called the winking star. Every 2 days, 20 hours, and 48 minutes, it drops in brightness over a period lasting 10 hours.

Meteor showers occur on the same nights each year as the Earth travels through areas in space that contain large amounts of dust and rock, often left by comets. Every year around August 11 and 12, a meteor shower called the Perseids can be seen originating from Perseus. Try watching a few days ahead and a few days after those dates so you don't miss it.

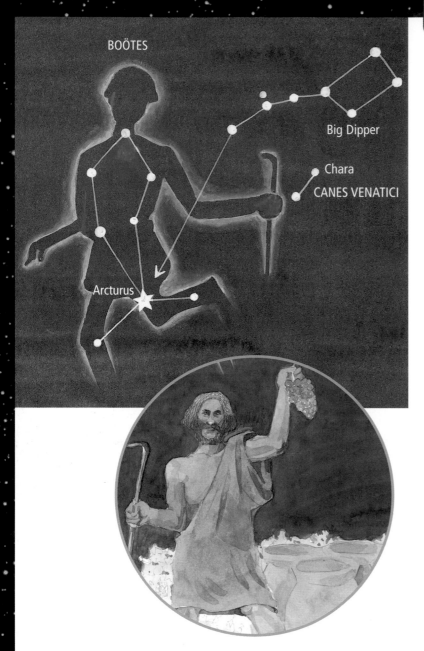

BOÖTES

Big Dipper

Chara

CANES VENATICI

Arcturus

Boötes
(boe-OH-teez)

The Herdsman
(spring)

Dionysus, the Greek god of wine, went to see a man called Icarius. Icarius was such a fine host, Dionysus thanked him by teaching him how to grow grapes for making wine.

Icarius wanted to teach more people how to grow wine grapes, and he traveled out to the country, bringing wine for others to taste. When Icarius met some shepherds and shared his wine, he was careful to remind them to mix it with water before they drank. But the shepherds didn't listen to Icarius's instructions and drank the wine without mixing it.

By the next morning the men were so sick, they thought Icarius had tried to poison them. The shepherds chased after Icarius, then attacked and killed him.

When Dionysus found out what had happened, he was

so angry that he punished the shepherds by placing a plague upon the land. Icarius was raised to the sky and honored as the constellation Boötes.

Where Is It?

You can find Boötes by starting at the handle of the Big Dipper. There is a useful saying: "Arc to Arcturus and speed on to Spica."

Instead of connecting the dots in a straight line, follow a curved line extending from the handle to the very bright star Arcturus. From this bright star, you can discover the outline of Boötes. Then look on the Constellation Chart to "speed on to Spica" and find the constellation Virgo.

A Closer Look

- The Greeks thought Boötes's job was to make sure the bear followed its path around the pole, for if the bear left the path, people would not know their directions.

- At 37 light years away, Arcturus is one of the closest bright stars, as well as one of the brightest stars in the spring sky.

- Boötes's two dogs, Asterion and Chara, are found in the constellation Canes Venatici, the Hunting Dogs. Boötes kept them on a leash as he hunted for the two bears, Ursa Major and Ursa Minor.

- Ancient Egyptians thought the northern stars that circled the celestial pole were evil, and the great bear one of the most dangerous. They believed Boötes was placed there to make sure the bear did not cause any trouble on Earth.

- A long time ago, people thought Arcturus was responsible for drought and disease.

CORONA BOREALIS

Alphecca

BOÖTES

Arcturus

The Northern Crown
(summer)

The story of the Northern Crown also starts with Dionysus, the Greek god of wine. Dionysus wanted to marry Princess Ariadne, the daughter of King Minos, who ruled the island of Crete. When Dionysus proposed, Ariadne said no because she thought he was only a mortal.

To prove he was a god, Dionysus took off his crown and threw it up into the sky. Seeing the crown turn to stars convinced Ariadne that he was a god. The princess married Dionysus and became immortal too.

In another version of this myth, King Minos kept a vile monster called the Minotaur. The half-bull, half-man creature lived in a maze from which it was impossible to escape, for anyone who entered was eaten by the monster.

Every year, King Minos forced the king of Athens to send him seven of the most handsome men and seven of the most beautiful maidens. He put them into the maze to be eaten by the Minotaur.

Theseus thought he could kill the monster, so he asked his father, the king of Athens, to let him go fight the Minotaur. His father was worried that Theseus would be killed, but gave him permission to go.

When King Minos's daughter saw Theseus, she fell in love with him at once. Secretly, the princess offered Theseus her help, on the condition that he take her back to Athens to become his bride. Theseus eagerly agreed, so Ariadne slipped him a small sword and a ball of thread before he was taken to the maze.

Theseus unwound the thread as he walked through the maze, knowing he could follow it to find his way out again. When the Minotaur attacked him, he used the sword to cut off its head. He followed the thread

A CLOSER LOOK

Corona Borealis has been called the Broken Platter because it is not completely round. In Australia, it is thought of as the Boomerang.

Alphecca is the brightest star in Corona Borealis. This white star is the Pearl of the Crown.

back to the entrance, and escaped with the others, taking Princess Ariadne with him.

On their way to Athens, they stopped at the island of Naxos. As Ariadne slept, the ungrateful Theseus went back to the ship and sailed home without her. He claimed that the goddess Minerva had visited him in a dream and commanded him to leave. When Ariadne woke up and realized Theseus was gone, she began to cry.

Aphrodite, the goddess of love, felt sorry for Ariadne. She promised the princess the love of an immortal, to replace the mortal who had deserted her.

The god Dionysus found Ariadne alone and crying. He was so enthralled with her beauty, he immediately asked her to marry him. He gave her a magnificent gold crown set with jewels for a wedding present. Ariadne enjoyed a happy life with Dionysus. When she died, Dionysus set the crown in the sky to honor his wife.

Where Is It?

Corona Borealis is a small constellation with many bright stars. It looks like a smile from a happy face. Connect the dots from the base of the triangle at the top of Boötes to reach the Northern Crown. You will easily spot the bright stars that form the half circle of Corona Borealis.

Space Notes

☆ Although interstellar means "between stars," interstellar space refers to the part of the universe beyond the solar system.

☆ The space between the stars in the Milky Way contains enough gas to create 20 billion stars like the Sun.

☆ Old, cool stars release cosmic dust—a type of soot made of graphite, which is the same material used in making pencils.

Cygnus
(SIG-nus)

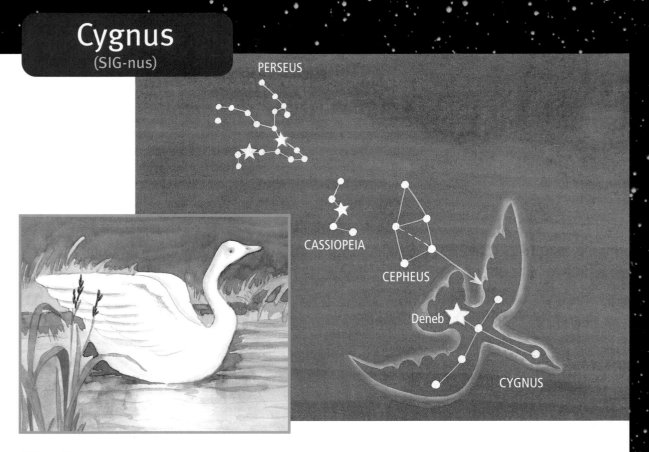

PERSEUS

CASSIOPEIA

CEPHEUS

Deneb

CYGNUS

The Swan
(summer)

There is more than one story about how Cygnus the swan came to be in the sky. One Greek myth tells about a great singer and musician named Orpheus. He played the lyre so well that even wild animals would come to hear the music. After his death, Orpheus was placed in the sky as a swan, near the stars of his lyre.

In another story, Phaëthon bragged to his friends that the early Greek sun god, Helios, was his father. His friends did not believe him, so to prove it Phaëthon asked Helios if he could drive the sun chariot across the sky for a day.

Helios said yes, reminding Phaëthon that he must stay halfway between Heaven and Earth. But Phaëthon was not listening to the advice of his father. First he steered too

☆ Stars at the center of the Milky Way galaxy travel more quickly than the ones farther out. Our sun takes about 240 million years to complete one orbit around the center of the galaxy. This is called a cosmic year. Our solar system has made about 20 orbits around the Milky Way.

☆ Our sun is about 4.6 million years old. In 5 billion years, the Sun will become a red giant, growing bigger and bigger. After it has used up its fuel, it will shrink into a white dwarf star, becoming smaller than the Earth.

high and burnt a streak of light in the sky that became known as the Milky Way. Then he rode too close to the Earth and singed it, drying up the rivers and lakes. A desert was formed in the land of Africa and all the people were burnt black.

Zeus, the king of the gods, realized that Phaëthon was destroying the Earth and hurled a thunderbolt to stop him. Phaëthon's body fell from the sky and landed in a river.

One of Phaëthon's friends, Cycnus, rushed to the bank to look for him. He dove deep into the river, and frantically swam back and forth, his movement through the water making him look like a swan. Cycnus was too late to save Phaëthon and became so upset over his friend's death that he died from grief. Helios felt sorry for Cycnus and put him in the sky as Cygnus, the swan.

Where Is It?

Cygnus, also called the Northern Cross, is located in a part of the Milky Way that divides into two (see the Constellation Chart). Follow the Milky Way from Perseus through Cassiopeia to Cygnus.

Another way to find Cygnus is by starting at the square part of Cepheus. Imagine a diagonal line connecting the top left star of the square to the bottom right star, then extend the line to reach the star that forms the wing of the swan.

A CLOSER LOOK

Many cultures have identified Cygnus as a bird, but not everyone has seen a swan. It has also been called a horned owl, an ibis, an eagle, and a hen.

Deneb, a white star in the swan's tail, is 63,000 times brighter than the Sun, but so far away it looks only like a very bright star.

Lyra
(LYE-ruh)

Deneb
Vega
LYRA
CYGNUS

The Lyre
(summer)

The Greek sun god Apollo, also the god of music, gave his son Orpheus a musical instrument called a lyre. Gods, animals, trees, and even mountains loved to listen to the music Orpheus made. The notes he played were so enchanting, they could not turn away when he played the lyre.

Orpheus fell deeply in love with a beautiful young woman named Eurydice. They had not been married very long when Eurydice was bitten by a poisonous snake and died. She went to Hades, the underworld — where mortals went when their lives on Earth were over.

Heartbroken, Orpheus followed her to Hades and tried to save her by charming the gods with his music. The gods were so enchanted by the sounds of his lyre, they agreed to let Eurydice leave with him on one condition. He must not look at her on the way out.

Poor Orpheus found it hard to be patient and could not resist looking at his wife before they were safe in the upper world. His heart broke for the second time as Eurydice faded away to remain in Hades forever.

Orpheus wandered the Earth, playing lonely music on his lyre. The music was still so beautiful that maidens followed him everywhere, begging him not to be so sad. They wanted him to marry again, but he would not even consider it.

After Orpheus's death, Zeus raised his lyre to the sky so that his music would become immortal.

Where Is It?

Lyra is located just outside the arm of the Milky Way. It can be spotted easily by imagining a line starting at the star Deneb, in Cygnus. Travel across Cygnus to the bright star Vega. This blue-white star in Lyra is sometimes called the Harp Star.

A CLOSER LOOK

The constellations of Cygnus, Lyra, and Aquila are near one another and form the summer triangle (see Aquila). Vega is the brightest star in the triangle.

In about 14,000 years, the north pole star will be Vega, which is six times brighter than Polaris, our current north star.

Aquila
(ah-KWILL-uh)

Deneb · Vega · summer triangle · LYRA · CYGNUS · Altair · AQUILA

The Eagle
(summer)

There are several Greek myths about the eagle, known as Aquila. In one story, the gods needed someone to bring them fresh nectar. The job of cup-bearer was considered a great honor and could not be performed by an ordinary mortal.

Zeus, the king of the gods, asked Aquila to fly down to

Earth, search for the most beautiful young person he could find, and bring the youth back to the Great Hall of the Gods.

Aquila immediately spread his long wings and soared away. His piercing eyes searched over mountains, valleys, forests, and plains. Day after day, Aquila eyed the people he saw on Earth, but could not find anyone worthy of being cup-bearer. Finally, soaring over a mountain range, Aquila spotted Ganymede, a shepherd caring for a flock of sheep. He was the most beautiful youth Aquila had ever seen.

Aquila folded his wings close to his body and dove toward the shepherd, slowing just enough to gently pick up the young man with his talons. Aquila was tired from the long search, but so devoted to Zeus that he did not even think about resting. The eagle flew up into the sky and beyond the clouds to Mount Olympus, with Ganymede dangling underneath.

Zeus was thrilled when he saw the handsome youth. To reward the eagle, he saved a place for Aquila in the stars when he died.

Another Greek myth that

A CLOSER LOOK

Altair is one of the brightest stars in the sky. It rotates once every six hours, which is so rapid that the star has developed a flattened shape. In contrast, our sun only rotates once every 28 days.

We know that Aquila has been recognized as a constellation at least since 1200 B.C. because it has been found on stone carvings.

Aquila has also been called the King of Birds and the Bird of Zeus.

Arab people have called this constellation the Flying Eagle, as well as the Crow or Raven.

The Persians had two different names for Aquila—the Star-striking Falcon and the Flying Vulture.

Aquila was known as the Hunting Eagle by the Turks.

includes Aquila is the story of Hermes, the messenger god, who fell in love with Aphrodite. No matter what Hermes tried, the goddess of love refused to even speak to him. Heartbroken, Hermes went to Zeus for help, claiming that he would die as a mortal if the beautiful Aphrodite would not agree to see him.

Zeus tried to convince Hermes that his love would fade, but the god's feelings grew more intense with each day that passed. Not knowing what else to do, Hermes went to Zeus again, begging even more desperately for help.

Zeus felt pity for the lovesick god, and had an idea that he thought might help. He turned to the great eagle, Aquila, and commanded him to fly to the river where Aphrodite was known to bathe. He told Aquila to steal one of Aphrodite's magic slippers off the shore while the goddess was in the water.

Aquila took off at once, flew to the shore of the river, and saw Aphrodite in the water. He swooped down to the river's edge and plucked a magic slipper from the sand. When Aquila returned to Zeus with the slipper, he gave it to Hermes, who happily used the slipper to force Aphrodite to see him. The goddess relented and they had a handsome son, whom they named after themselves—Hermaphroditus.

Where Is It?

To find Aquila, connect Deneb in Cygnus and Vega in Lyra to form a triangle to the bright star Altair, in Aquila. This star group is called the summer triangle. To find it, just remember, "Depart from Deneb, Voyage to Vega, and Arrive at Altair." Altair forms the eagle's head.

Space Notes

☆ Galaxies are made up of stars, dust, and gas pulled together by gravity.

☆ As far as we know, there are over 100 billion galaxies in the universe.

☆ Planets do not make their own light, but shine by reflecting light from the Sun.

☆ Although Venus is a planet, it is often called the morning or evening star. It appears bright because it passes so close to the Earth and because its white clouds reflect 72 percent of the Sun's light.

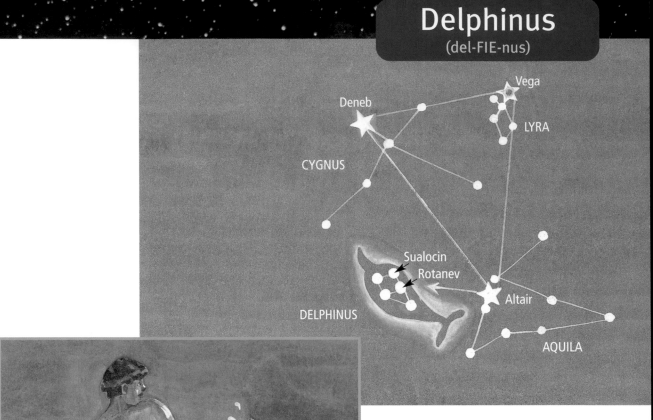

Delphinus
(del-FIE-nus)

Vega

Deneb

LYRA

CYGNUS

Sualocin
Rotanev

Altair

DELPHINUS

AQUILA

The Dolphin
(summer)

A mermaid named Amphitrite was hiding from the Greek sea god Poseidon, who wanted to marry her. A dolphin discovered her and told her not to flee from the god. She listened to the dolphin and married Poseidon, who was so happy that he raised the dolphin up to the heavens.

In another Greek story, a popular singer named Arion was

traveling across the sea. He was so talented that he had been given many prizes, including great amounts of money. The oarsmen on the boat wanted to steal it all from him, and decided to throw Arion in the water and leave him to drown.

One night, Arion had a dream about their plot and he made up a plan to save himself. When the oarsmen captured Arion, he asked if he could sing one last song before they threw him overboard.

After they agreed, Arion walked to the bow of the ship and began to sing. He had such a wonderful voice, all kinds of sea animals gathered around the boat to listen. Just before the song was over, Arion leaped off the boat and into the water.

A dolphin caught Arion on his back, then brought him safely to the shore.

Apollo, the god of the sun and music, was so glad that the dolphin had saved the talented singer, he rewarded the dolphin by placing him in the stars.

Where Is It?

Delphinus is on the opposite side of the Milky Way from Lyra. Find the summer triangle (see Aquila for directions) and go to the most southerly bright star, Altair, in Aquila. Delphinus is just to the east of Altair.

Look for about five bright stars very close together. Four of the stars make the diamond shape of a kite, with the next closest star forming the tail.

Space Notes

☆ Stars are made up of two main gases, hydrogen and helium.

☆ The largest stars are called supergiants and are 100,000 times bigger than the Sun. The smallest stars are smaller than the Earth.

☆ Some stars die by blowing up in a tremendous explosion called a supernova. The core that is left after the explosion may become a black hole, with gravity so strong that anything nearby is sucked into it forever. It is black because even light is drawn into it.

A CLOSER LOOK

Delphinus was once called the Riding Camel by Arabs, and the Cross of Jesus by early Christians.

The brightest star in Delphinus is called Sualocin, which is

Nicolaus spelled backwards. The second brightest star is a double star called Rotanev which spells Venator backwards. Nicolaus Venator is the Latin name of an astronomer.

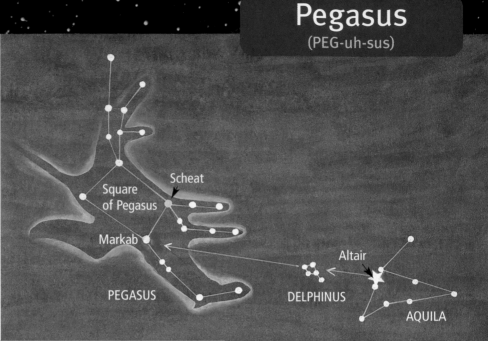

Scheat

Square of Pegasus

Markab

PEGASUS

Altair

DELPHINUS

AQUILA

The Winged Horse
(autumn)

When Perseus cut off the head of Medusa and flew over the ocean, her blood dripped into the sea. The Greek sea god Poseidon felt the drops and knew they were from Medusa, for he had been in love with her when she was a beautiful woman. He remembered what Medusa had been like before she was turned into a monster.

Poseidon took some of the drops of blood, mixed them

with the foamy bubbles of the ocean's waves, then added white sand from the beach. Out of this mixture came Pegasus, the winged horse.

Another Greek myth tells of Bellerophon, the prince of Corinth, who was an expert at taming horses. He desperately wanted to ride Pegasus, but the horse was so wild, even Bellerophon could not get near him. One night, Bellerophon fell asleep in the temple of Athena, the goddess of arts, crafts, and war. He dreamt that Athena gave him a magical golden bridle that could be used to tame Pegasus. When Bellerophon opened his eyes the next morning, he was thrilled to discover he was holding a real golden bridle.

Filled with excitement at the prospect of riding the handsome Pegasus, Bellerophon kept the golden bridle with him until he found Pegasus, drinking at a spring. Without making a sound, Bellerophon crept closer and closer to the winged horse, until with a sudden movement he threw the bridle over the animal's head. Pegasus immediately lost all his wildness, and stood patiently while Bellerophon climbed upon his back. With a nudge, Bellerophon steered Pegasus swiftly upwards.

Delighted with his new way of traveling, Bellerophon rode Pegasus to Lycia, where a ferocious creature called the Chimera was terrifying the

A CLOSER LOOK

- The Great Square of Pegasus is an asterism—a part of a constellation.

- The winged horse has been found on coins made in 4 B.C.

- The brightest star in Pegasus is a white star called Markab, and the second brightest is the yellow star, Scheat.

kingdom. The Chimera's skin was so tough, it could not be hurt by any blade. Flaming torrents of fire shot out of the Chimera's three heads—one a roaring lion, the next a bleating goat, the third a hissing serpent.

Careful not to let Pegasus get burned, Bellerophon flew as close as he could to the flaming Chimera. He carried a spear with a great lump of lead on the tip. When he thrust the spear into the lion's mouth, the lead melted and flowed into the beast's stomach. The Chimera was poisoned by the lead and died.

The king of Lycia was so pleased, he allowed Bellerophon to marry his daughter and inherit his kingdom. Bellerophon was a popular king, but so proud of his success that he became conceited enough to compare himself to the gods.

Bellerophon decided to enter Olympus on the back of Pegasus, but as they flew upward, Pegasus bucked him off his back. Bellerophon landed on a thistle bed in a distant country, where he walked aimlessly as a beggar until his death. Zeus allowed Pegasus to enter Olympus, and made the horse the carrier of his thunderbolts.

Where Is It?

Pegasus is a large constellation, with part of it composed of four bright stars that form a square. To find it, start at Altair in Aquila and travel right through Delphinus. Continue east into the Great Square of Pegasus.

Space Notes

☆ Some stars look bright because they are closer to us, while other stars that appear brilliant may be farther away but burn more brightly.

☆ Stars are not close to each other in space, but look that way because they share the same part of the sky we see.

☆ At least half of the stars we see have companion stars. Two closely spaced stars, called binaries, are held in each other's gravity and orbit one another. Other stars, called optical doubles, may appear close together, but are actually just in the same line of site.

Taurus
(TOR-us)

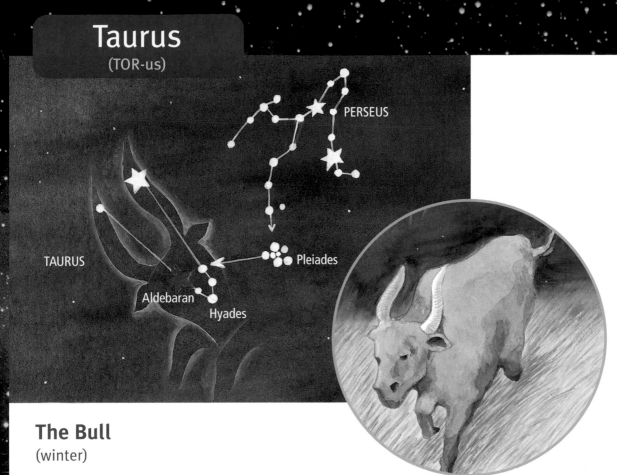

PERSEUS

TAURUS

Pleiades

Aldebaran

Hyades

The Bull
(winter)

One Greek myth associated with Taurus tells the story of Europa, daughter of the king of Tyre. Zeus, the king of the gods, had fallen in love with Europa, but was unable to get near her because she was never alone. The king's servants guarded the princess so carefully that Zeus changed himself into a bull. He wandered among the king's cattle, which were eating grass in a field by the ocean.

As Europa walked along the shore, she glanced into the field and noticed the handsome white bull with golden horns. She wanted to have a better look at the princely animal and walked up, holding out some grass for it to eat. The bull was so good-natured and tame that Europa grabbed hold of the horns and climbed up onto the bull's back.

Carefully the bull ambled closer and closer to the water's edge. When he was near enough, the bull bolted into the water, and began swimming towards the island of Crete. Europa did not dare let go of the bull until they reached land.

When they arrived at Crete, Zeus changed into his human form. Together they had three sons who grew up to be kings—Minos, Sarpedon, and Rhadamanthus. Minos and Rhadamanthus became judges of the dead in the underworld.

Another Greek myth that relates to Taurus is the story of the Pleiades, the seven sisters that form the left shoulder of the constellation Taurus. Orion, the hunter, fell in love with all of the sisters. This upset their father, Atlas, the god who held the Earth on his shoulders. To keep them apart, Zeus placed the bull between the sisters and the hunter. Eventually all of the sisters married gods except the seventh, who married a mortal. She was ashamed of herself,

A Closer Look

- The name of the continent of Europe may come from the mythical Europa.

- The V-shaped cluster of stars that forms the face of the bull is called the Hyades. After Ursa Major, this star group is the second closest cluster to the Earth, at only 150 light years away.

- Ancient Chinese called the Hyades the Golden Ox.

- The bright red star Aldebaran forms the right eye of Taurus. Aldebaran, meaning "the follower," trails the Pleiades through the night.

- Taurus is one of the 12 constellations that make up the zodiac. The zodiac is an imaginary circle in the sky, divided into the 12 constellations where the Sun, Moon, and planets appear to travel. The 12 constellations, called the signs of the zodiac, were known to the Babylonians by 450 B.C.

- The other signs of the zodiac are the constellations Aries, Gemini, Cancer, Leo, Virgo, Libra, Scorpio, Sagittarius, Capricorn, Aquarius, and Pisces.

and that is why her star is the hardest to see.

A Polynesian myth explains that the Pleiades began as one immense and breathtaking star. The star told everyone that she was the most dazzling star in the entire sky. She bragged so often, the other stars became tired of her and begged the god Tane to make her be quiet. After much thought, he picked up the star Aldebaran and hurled it at the boastful star. Aldebaran was thrilled to be chosen for this job, and was not hurt at all when he smashed into her. The single star broke into six smaller stars, who still boast, but now do it quietly, whispering that they are even lovelier than before, now that there are six of them.

Where Is It?

Connect the dots from Perseus to the Pleiades, and on to the rest of Taurus, the bull. Taurus is an easy constellation to imagine if you remember you are only looking at his front half. The rest of him is underwater, as he swims to Crete. The bull also looks as if he might be backing away from Orion's raised club.

Many people who inspect the Pleiades can only spot six stars, so if you can see the seventh you have very good eyesight. If you look through binoculars at the star cluster Pleiades, you can see about 50 stars, but if you look through a telescope, you may see 400 to 500 stars.

Space Notes

☆ Although they seldom twinkle, planets look a lot like stars. How can you tell the difference? Stars appear to stay in one spot, while the planets wander. If you are looking at a planet on different nights, the planet will be in a different location compared to the constellations around it. If you look through binoculars or a telescope, you may be able to see the shape of a planet, but the appearance of a star will barely change.

☆ Planets are not included on star charts because their locations are always changing as they orbit the sun.

☆ All the planets except Pluto can be found in or near the constellations of the zodiac. Mercury, Mars, Venus, Jupiter, and Saturn can be seen with the naked eye. Jupiter and Venus are brighter than stars.

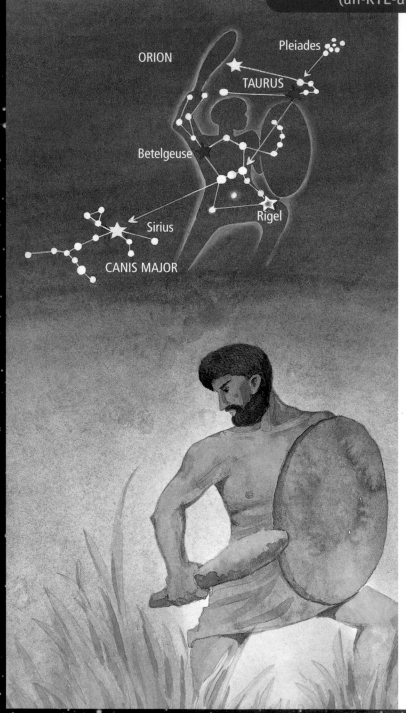

The Hunter
(winter)

In Greek mythology, Orion was a famous hunter and warrior. He bragged that he could kill any animal on Earth, but being brave did not protect him from the scorpion. The mighty Orion died after battling with a giant scorpion who stung his heel. Orion and the Scorpion are placed at opposite ends of the sky so they will not fight again.

In another story, Orion fell in love with Merope, daughter of King Oenopion. The king pretended that he would allow Orion to marry his daughter, but instead forced the giant to put off their wedding plans. Over and over, King Oenopion gave Orion difficult tasks to perform, insisting that the giant prove himself worthy of his daughter.

Finally, Orion realized that the king would never let them marry. He made plans to steal Merope away, but the king's guards caught him. King Oenopion was so angry, he put Orion into a deep sleep. While the giant slumbered, the king caused him to go blind, then left the giant to fend for himself by the sea.

The blind giant heard the sound of hammering and walked toward it until he came upon Hephaestus, the blacksmith god. Hephaestus felt sorry for Orion and offered him the help of one of his servants. Orion knew he could get his sight back if he traveled to the home of Apollo, the sun god. He told the servant to guide him toward the east, until they reached the land where the Sun rose. Facing the dawn, Orion felt the warmth of the Sun on his face and was able to see again.

Orion traveled to the island of Crete where he fell in love with Artemis, the goddess of the Moon. Her job was to drive the moon chariot across the sky, but because she was spending so much time with Orion she did not do her job. Her brother Apollo told her to stop neglecting the Moon, but Artemis ignored him and Apollo became angry.

A CLOSER LOOK

Orion has been called many names, including the Warrior, the Light of Heaven, the Foot-Turning Wanderer, and the Madman.

Many stars look white with the naked eye, but bright stars such as red Betelgeuse and bluish-white Rigel can be seen in color.

The name Betelgeuse means "shoulder or armpit of the central one," which refers to the star's location in Orion, as well as Orion's position among bright neighboring constellations. Betelgeuse shines with the brightness of 18,000 Suns.

The bright star below and to the right of Orion's belt is Rigel, the seventh brightest star in the sky. Rigel is actually a double star. The two bluish-white stars appear as one, unless you are looking through a telescope.

The three bright stars that form Orion's belt have been called the Golden Grains, the Golden Walnuts, the Arrow, the Magi, and the Three Kings.

Look for a fuzzy star just below the belt. It is the Orion Nebula—a "stellar nursery" where new stars are formed. A new star is born in our galaxy every 18 days.

As Orion bathed in the sea one day, Apollo used his power to shield the giant in light. He challenged Artemis to shoot an arrow into the patch of light. She could not resist showing off and immediately shot an arrow into the water where Orion was bathing.

When the waves brought Orion's body to the shore, Artemis was heartbroken. She pulled him into her chariot and took him to the darkest part of the sky, where his stars would look the brightest.

Where Is It?

There are several ways to find Orion. Connect the dots from the Pleiades, through the rest of Taurus to Orion. You can also find Orion by watching Cassiopeia. When the Queen is high in the sky, look eastward where Orion will be rising.

The three stars of Orion's belt are spaced close together and are almost equally bright. You will soon be able to spot Orion just by looking up from the horizon.

Follow the stars in the belt down to the brightest star in the sky—Sirius in Canis Major. Canis Major and Canis Minor were Orion's hunting dogs.

Space Notes

☆ Clouds of dust and gas in space are called nebulae. Inside the nebulae, gravity pulls together gas and dust particles into smaller clouds that contract, spin, and release heat. Over tens of thousands of years, stars are formed, with slow spinners forming a single star. Fast spinners create double stars, while medium spinners such as our sun may produce planets.

☆ Stars the size of the Sun take 20 million years to start shining steadily after they form. It takes this long for the gas cloud to contract enough to raise the temperature and pressure sufficiently for the hydrogen to form helium. The stars then release energy as heat and light.

Astronomy: A Hobby for Life

The sky is like a huge, sparkling map made out of pictures. Now you know the location of at least 15 constellations on the map, making the nighttime sky more familiar and more incredible at the same time.

It is remarkable to think you are looking at the same stars, in the same patterns, as people who lived on Earth thousands of years before you. Over several tens of thousands of years, some constellation patterns will become noticeably different, but you will not be able to see a difference in your lifetime.

Keep a list of all the constellations you have been able to locate. If you go on a trip, remember to look at the night sky. The constellations may stay the same, or may appear to be in a different part of the sky, depending on how far you travel.

Finding constellations is a hobby you can do alone or share with others. You can lie out on a blanket in the backyard to look for patterns in the sky, search for bright stars from the back seat of the car on a long drive, or watch for meteors from your bedroom window. Wherever you are, there are always constellations to see and many stories to explain how they came to be.

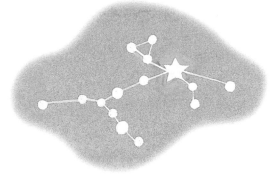

Space Notes

☆ Stars rise four minutes earlier every night and about an hour earlier every two weeks. They rise a day earlier over the whole year.

☆ If you want to see the stars that will be visible in the early evening of the next season, just stay up later. The stars of the next season can be observed at about midnight, with the stars of the following season visible by about 4:00 a.m.

Checklist of Constellations

All of the constellations below are visible from most parts of the northern hemisphere. Constellations described as circumpolar are visible year round from most parts of Canada, but will become seasonal at lower latitudes. (The best viewing seasons for more southerly locations are given in parentheses.)

Constellation	Description	Best Early Evening Viewing
Andromeda	Maiden	Autumn
Antlia	Air Pump	Spring
Aquarius	Water Carrier	Autumn
Aquila	Eagle	Summer
Ara	Altar	Spring
Aries	Ram	Autumn
Auriga	Charioteer	Winter
Boötes	Herdsman	Spring
Caelum	Engraving Tool	Winter
Camelopardalis	Giraffe	Circumpolar (fall/winter)
Cancer	Crab	Spring
Canes Venatici	Hunting Dogs	Spring
Canis Major	Great Dog	Winter
Canis Minor	Little Dog	Winter
Capricorn	Sea Goat	Summer
Carina	Keel	Winter
Cassiopeia	Queen	Circumpolar (fall)
Cepheus	King	Circumpolar (fall)
Centaurus	Centaur	Spring
Cetus	Sea Monster	Autumn
Columba	Dove	Winter
Coma Berenices	Berenice's Hair	Spring
Corona Borealis	Northern Crown	Summer
Corvus	Crow	Spring

Constellation	Description	Best Early Evening Viewing
Crater	Cup	Spring
Cygnus	Swan	Summer
Delphinus	Dolphin	Summer
Draco	Dragon	Circumpolar (summer)
Equuleus	Little Horse	Summer
Eridanus	River	Winter
Gemini	Twins	Winter
Hercules	Hercules	Summer
Horologium	Clock	Winter
Hydra	Sea Serpent	Spring
Indus	Indian	Summer
Lacerta	Lizard	Autumn
Leo	Lion	Spring
Leo Minor	Little Lion	Spring
Lepus	Hare	Winter
Libra	Scales	Spring
Lynx	Lynx	Spring
Lyra	Harp	Summer
Monoceros	Unicorn	Winter
Ophiuchus	Serpent Holder	Summer
Orion	Hunter	Winter
Pegasus	Winged Horse	Autumn
Perseus	Hero	Circumpolar (winter)
Piscis Austrinus	Southern Fish	Autumn
Pisces	Fish	Autumn
Puppis	Stern	Winter
Pyxis	Mariner's Compass	Spring
Sagitta	Arrow	Summer
Sagittarius	Archer	Summer
Scorpio	Scorpion	Summer
Sculptor	Sculptor's Studio	Autumn
Scutum	Shield	Summer

Constellation	Description	Best Early Evening Viewing
Serpens Caput	Serpent's Head	Summer
Serpens Cauda	Serpent's Tail	Summer
Sextans	Sextant	Spring
Taurus	Bull	Winter
Triangulum	Triangle	Autumn
Ursa Major	Great Bear	Circumpolar (spring)
Ursa Minor	Little Bear	Circumpolar (spring/summer)
Virgo	Virgin	Spring
Vulpecula	Little Fox	Summer

Once you are familiar with some of the featured star groups, use the chart on the opposite page to connect the dots to other constellations visible from the northern hemisphere. Remember, what you see will depend on your location and the time of year.

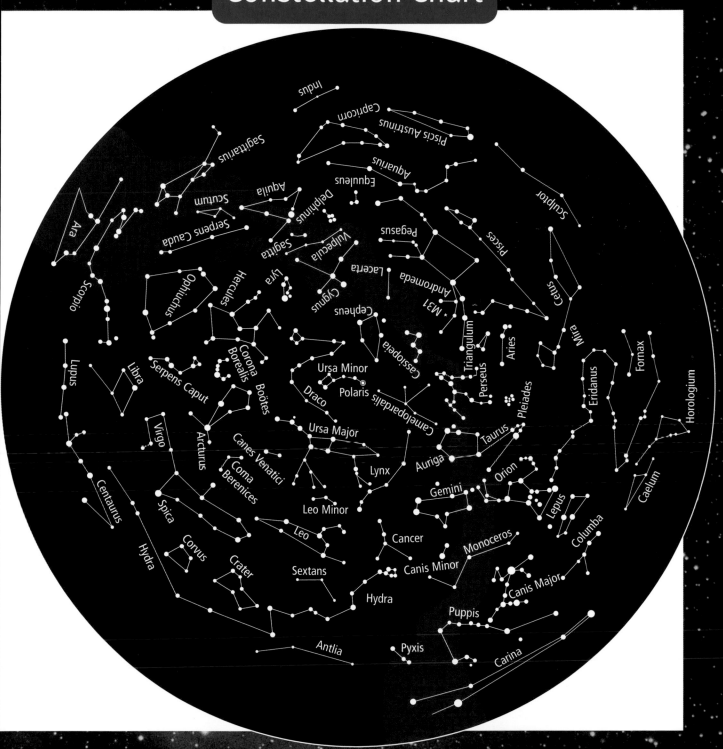

Glossary

Andromeda galaxy a spiral galaxy that is $1^1/_2$ times as wide as the Milky Way galaxy and about $2^1/_2$ million light years away. It contains about 400 billion stars and is the most distant object visible to the naked eye.

asterism a group of stars that forms part of a constellation.

astronomer a person who studies astronomy.

astronomy the science of studying celestial bodies, including distance, brightness, size, motion, position, and composition.

atmospheric extinction the apparent dimming of stars and other celestial objects, due to scattering and absorption of light in the Earth's atmosphere.

axis an imaginary line through the center of a celestial object, around which the object turns. The line forming the Earth's axis goes through the north and south poles.

binary stars two closely spaced stars that are held in each other's gravity and revolve around one another.

black hole a collapsed celestial object with such strong gravity that anything nearby, including light, is sucked into it forever.

celestial relating to the sky.

circumpolar constellations constellations near a celestial pole, which do not appear to rise or set, but instead appear to circle the celestial pole.

circumpolar stars stars near a celestial pole, which do not appear to rise or set, but instead appear to circle the celestial pole.

comet a celestial object of ice, rock, and dust that orbits the Sun. When comets pass near the Sun, they develop a tail of gas and dust that points away from the Sun.

companion stars. *See* binary stars.

cone cells cells in the center of the retina that help you to see things in color and fine detail.

constellation a group of stars that represents an imaginary figure and belongs to one of the 88 officially recognized star patterns, used to define different areas of the sky.

cosmic year the time it takes our sun to complete one orbit around the center of the Milky Way galaxy, about 240 million years.

double stars. *See* binary stars.

equator an imaginary circle around a planet or moon that divides the north and south hemispheres, halfway between the north and south poles.

falling star. *See* meteor.

fireball a brilliant meteor.

galaxy a group of stars, dust, and gas pulled together by gravity.

gravity the force that causes objects to fall or to be pulled toward another object.

guard stars the two stars on the opposite side from the Little Dipper's handle.

interstellar between stars.

interstellar space the part of the universe beyond the solar system.

latitude the distance of a location north or south of the Earth's equator, measured in degrees.

light pollution an inefficient use of light that illuminates areas other than those intended, such as the sky rather than the ground. The glare and excessive brightness can make it difficult to view faint celestial objects.

light year the unit used to measure how far light can travel through space in one year, equaling 9.46 trillion kilometres (5.88 trillion miles).

magnitude a measurement of the brightness of a celestial object. A first magnitude star is brighter than a fifth magnitude star.

meteor a streak of light seen in the sky, caused by fragments of rock and dust burning up as they enter the Earth's atmosphere. Meteors are also called falling stars or shooting stars.

meteorite a meteor that hits the surface of a planet or moon.

meteor shower when a larger than normal number of meteors enter the atmosphere during a short period of time and appear to come from the same area of sky.

Milky Way galaxy the name of the galaxy where the Earth is located, which appears as a band of light seen across the night sky. It is about 100,000 light years across and contains some 200 billion stars.

moon the natural satellite of a planet. The Earth's satellite is called the Moon, while other planets' moons are given individual names (such as Phobos and Deimos for the two small moons of Mars).

myth a story used to explain an event, practice, belief, or natural occurrence.

nebula a cloud of dust and gas within a galaxy, where new stars are formed.

northern hemisphere the half of the Earth that is north of the equator.

north pole the northernmost point of the Earth.

North Star the star almost directly above the north pole, and to which the axis of the Earth's north geographic pole points (currently Polaris).

observatory a building furnished with telescopes and other equipment for studying astronomy.

optical doubles stars that appear close together, but are actually just in the same line of site.

planet a celestial object of rock or gas that orbits a star. Planets do not produce light, but shine by reflecting the light of a star.

pointer stars the two stars on the side of the bowl away from the Big Dipper's handle (Dubhe and Merak), used as guides to point to the North Star.

pole star a star that is located directly above the Earth's pole. *See also* North Star.

precession the slow gyration, or wobble, of the Earth's axis, caused by the gravitational attraction of the Sun and Moon.

red giant an old star whose surface is cooling as it expands, later contracting to become a white dwarf.

retina an area at the back of the eyeball that receives images formed by the lens of the eye.

rod cells cells that are primarily on the outer edge of the retina, and are more sensitive to faint light and movement.

satellite objects that orbit a planet or moon. The Moon is a satellite of the Earth. Natural satellites are celestial objects, while artificial satellites are placed into orbit by scientists.

shooting star. *See* meteor.

solar system a star and the celestial bodies that orbit it. Our solar system includes the Sun, comets, millions of asteroids, more than 60 moons, and the 9 planets (Mercury, Venus, Earth, Mars, Jupiter, Saturn, Uranus, Neptune, and Pluto).

star a hot sphere of glowing gas that emits energy and light, like our sun.

star cluster a group of stars close to each other in space and born at the same time, out of the same material.

stellar nursery a nebula (cloud and dust within a galaxy) where stars are being formed.

summer triangle a triangle formed by connecting three bright stars: Vega, in the constellation Lyra; Deneb, in Cygnus; and Altair, in Aquila.

sun a star. The star at the center of our solar system is referred to as the Sun.

supergiant a very bright star and the largest known type of star.

supernova the huge, bright explosion of a star.

variable star a star that changes brightness, usually over a somewhat regular cycle.

white dwarf a small, faint, dense, and hot star near the end of its life.

zodiac an imaginary circle in the sky, divided into the 12 constellations where the Sun, Moon, and planets appear to travel. The constellations, or signs, of the zodiac are Aries, Taurus, Gemini, Cancer, Leo, Virgo, Libra, Scorpio, Sagittarius, Capricorn, Aquarius, and Pisces.

Index

Bold numbers refer to illustrations.

About the Author and Illustrators

Joan Hinz lives near Edmonton, Alberta. She has contributed to numerous publications, including *The Edmonton Journal*, *Alberta Venture* magazine, and various government websites. Her freelance work also entails producing stories for CBC Radio One, speech writing, and multimedia projects. This is her first book.

Joan's website at www.joanhinz.com contains additional author information, astronomy links, and fun for kids.

Illustrators

Chao Yu and Jue Wang are graduates of the Shandong University of Fine Arts in China. Together, they have contributed illustrations to more than 30 books in Canada and China. This is their first astronomy book.